# IMAGES
## *of America*

# FORT HOOD IN
# WORLD WAR II

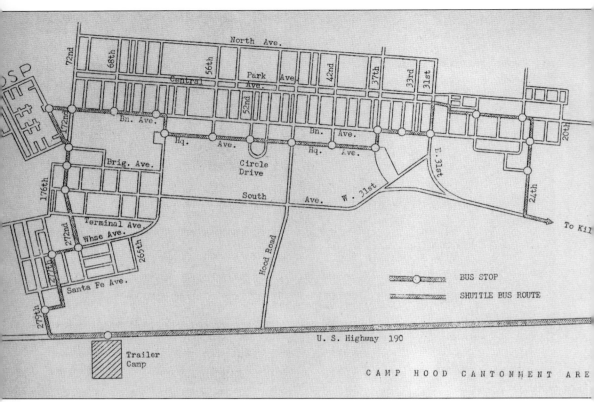

This 1942 diagram shows the street design for the original cantonment of Camp Hood. This cantonment would soon be called the South Camp, after the construction of the north cantonment eight months later. (From the author's collection.)

**ON THE COVER:** A tank destroyer crew takes part in mobilization training at Camp Hood's dry railroad. Part of the emphasis of tank destroyer training is mobility in the field. This training included the tricky loading and unloading of heavy equipment from railcars that were barely wider than the vehicles. An M10 gun motor carriage is shown here. (From the author's collection.)

IMAGES
*of America*

# FORT HOOD IN WORLD WAR II

David Ford

ARCADIA
PUBLISHING

Published by Arcadia Publishing
Charleston, South Carolina

Printed in the United States of America

Library of Congress Control Number: 2015950706

For all general information, please contact Arcadia Publishing:
Telephone 843-853-2070
Fax 843-853-0044
E-mail sales@arcadiapublishing.com
For customer service and orders:
Toll-Free 1-888-313-2665

Visit us on the Internet at www.arcadiapublishing.com

*To all the soldiers and civilians who worked and trained at Camp Hood.*

# Contents

# ACKNOWLEDGMENTS

The idea for this book was born with the discovery of Charles M. Thirlkeld's personal photo album. Thirlkeld was a steady force at Camp Hood during World War II as the post commander. He saw several commanding generals come and go as he kept the camp running smoothly. Without his collection, this book would not have been possible.

I would also like to express my gratitude to the people at Tank Destroyer.net for all the hard work, dedication, and effort they put into scanning the many Camp Hood newspapers that provided me with all kinds of great details I would have never found otherwise. Thanks also to Rob Haldeman and Lori Trill.

All photographs in this book are from my personal collection unless otherwise noted.

# INTRODUCTION

Army recruits quickly learn in basic training that a camp is a semipermanent base meant to be disbanded when it is no longer needed, and that a fort is an Army base with a permanent status. Fort Hood officially began as Camp Hood on September 18, 1942. Camp Hood was one of many Army camps that sprang up across the United States at an incredible rate as the military expanded fortyfold to prepare for World War II. Camp Hood was born out of a need to create tank destroyers, an answer to the German Panzer divisions that were so effective in the blitzkrieg across Europe.

Prior to the official opening of Camp Hood in September 1942, soldiers began arriving in the Killeen, Texas, area in early spring of that year. There was no real post or base to house the soldiers, so they bivouacked in tents and in any available space as the camp was built around them. The camp was symbolically opened in September with the raising of the giant garrison flag, measuring 20 feet by 38 feet. The flag was raised over a neat grid of gravel and dirt roads that connected a vast complex of quickly constructed, whitewashed, wood-frame buildings. Even after the official opening, many soldiers continued to live in tents and hotel rooms as the last of the barracks were being constructed. The camp opened with much fanfare, and Secretary of War Robert Patterson delivered the opening address. Patterson presented the official black-and-orange tank destroyer emblem, depicting a panther crunching a tank in its jaws. He also introduced the official tank destroyer motto, "Seek, Strike, and Destroy." This motto emphasized the notion that speed and mobility were key in tank warfare. During battle, tank destroyers would remain behind the lines in reserve. When a Panzer attack became evident, they would rush to the scene at high speed and destroy the Panzers in a fast-moving battle.

The Department of War named the camp after Gen. John Bell Hood. Hood's name was short, easily remembered, and had a strong local connection, as General Hood was the commander of the famed Civil War Texas Brigade. His son John B. Hood Jr. was present during the opening ceremonies. With the newly conceived Tank Destroyer Tactical and Firing Center beginning operations, the antitank doctrine and training quickly evolved. Antitank doctrine for the US Army was a concept that was as fresh and new as the white paint on the Camp Hood buildings.

The German army's blitzkrieg across France in the spring of 1940 stunned the world's military planners. Germany's infantry and armored divisions easily pushed through the French army and the British Expeditionary Force. As the Allied forces were regrouping in England in June 1940, US Army leadership sensed the growing possibility of facing the German army and its elite armored tank divisions. The Army hosted an antitank conference on April 15, 1941, to address the issue of the German armor threat. The conference failed to establish a consensus, due to the continued division of branch authority over antitank matters. Army chief of staff Gen. George C. Marshall took matters into his own hands and assigned Lt. Col. Andrew D. Bruce to be in charge of a small group to address the matter. Bruce would quickly become the Army's voice on all things antitank. It became evident that America was not ready for the German tanks, as very few artillerymen charged with antitank defense had ever seen a real tank in action. After many tests and deliberations, on November 27, 1941, a War Department letter ordered the activation of 53 tank destroyer battalions under the direct control of general headquarters. To help consolidate the antitank effort, the War Department issued a directive on December 3, 1941, to all commanding generals of all armies and groups concerning the inactivation of all antitank platoons, batteries, and troops in cavalry, infantry, and artillery units. The eight infantry antitank battalions were designated "tank destroyer" battalions. With this decree, the tank destroyer was born. The same letter also specified the creation of a Tank Destroyer Tactical and Firing Center. The creation of a new quasi-branch of the Army greatly expedited the development of antitank doctrine. The search was on for a fitting location for the tank destroyer home. There was to be little respite for the newly formed tank destroyers, as they would receive their baptism by fire in North Africa against Gen. Erwin Rommel's combat-hardened and experienced Afrika Korps in a few short months.

The soldiers assigned to the antitank mission were going to need to learn how to maneuver tank destroyers over difficult terrain in all types of hazardous conditions. Large training grounds were needed to allow the armored vehicles to roam and be able to fire at targets hundreds of yards away. Texas provided the ideal locale, with its wide-open spaces and gently rolling hills. On December 20, 1941, a contingent led by Lieutenant Colonel Bruce toured the Killeen, Texas, area. By January 10, 1942, barely one month after the attack on Pearl Harbor, Killeen was announced by Bruce as the location of the new tank destroyer training center. There was no time for hesitation; the new tank destroyer advance echelon moved quickly to establish the camp. On April 2, 1942, the 893rd Tank Destroyer Battalion arrived at Killeen from Fort Meade to begin training. By September 18, 1942, Camp Hood was officially opened. Local community members of Bell, Coryell, and Lampasas Counties met with military officers to discuss the impact on the area. The county officials helped in determining housing issues, rents, and the all-important acquisition of land. In only eight months, 108,000 acres were purchased and one of the most innovative—and, at times, controversial—combat training centers in the Army had been created. This acquisition of land was not without difficulties. To obtain the land, approximately 300 family homesteads and ranches were uprooted and moved. Some families gave up land that had been in the family for many generations. Many communities, such as Clear Creek, Elijah, Sugarloaf, and Antelope, vanished as the camp was created. Killeen swelled as the influx of workers quickly overwhelmed the small town. Extra bedrooms, porches, attics, chicken coops, and any other spaces that could provide a semblance of privacy were rented out. As the local cotton gins disappeared, a new industry sprang up around Killeen, Gatesville, and Copperas Cove: the Army.

Camp Hood was to be the epicenter of all things antitank. This included the training of individuals, activation of units, creation of doctrine, and development of antitank weapons and equipment. The tank destroyer unit's motto, "Seek, Strike, Destroy," and the esprit de corps the motto instills, would soon be passed on to the men grinding through the rigorous schooling at the training center. As Camp Hood reached its peak population of approximately 95,000, the nexus of the facility's establishment became the Unit Training Center. The center provided the advanced, specialized training that made a soldier a tank destroyer man. The Tank Destroyer School peaked on December 31, 1942, with a maximum attendance of 4,810 students. There were 12 Officer Candidate School classes, 9 officer courses, and 24 enlisted courses. All tank destroyer battalions were formed and organized by the Unit Training Center. Tank battalions were created from different Army branches. The battalions formed from infantry divisions were numbered in the 600s, those from armored divisions in the 700s, and those from field artillery in the 800s. By World War II, the training regimen at Camp Hood was of the highest standard and, at times, very cutting edge. Many innovative techniques created at the training center were copied at other centers within the Army. The tank-hunting course was the best example of advanced training. For the first time, live fire was used by the Army in training at Camp Hood. A full-scale mock town, dubbed the "Nazi Village," was built alongside a miniature replica of the village to be used for what is now termed urban warfare instruction. State-of-the-art gunnery ranges and open fields with varied terrain augmented the training. Even underground tunnels were built to provide dark shooting environments, to help with the interesting method of aiming by hearing. Tank destroyer soldiers would become well known for their shooting accuracy. Gunnery scores were a very popular topic in the camp newspaper, the *Hood Panther*.

Army Field Manual 18-5 was conceived and published by the Tank Destroyer Board resident at Camp Hood on June 16, 1942. FM 18-5, the official tank destroyer doctrine, was controversial and often misunderstood from its first day of printing. While the manual was developed under his command, General Bruce was not completely satisfied with one particular feature: tank destroyer battalions were not allowed to be integrated organically into the divisions to which they were assigned. Bruce felt that the tank destroyer battalions would be preyed upon as replacements to units on the front line. He was correct in this suspicion, as most tank destroyer battalions were broken up and dispersed in the field. One of the most significant issues facing deployed tank destroyer battalions was the lack of familiarity of tank destroyer doctrine by the rest of the Army. Good radio communications, road priority, and a high level of coordination was required to properly execute tank destroyer tactics. A program was initiated on November 30, 1942, for Army generals and general staff to train them in tank destroyer methods. This program did little to sway field commanders to the tank destroyer doctrine.

Soldiers were not the only people to pass through the camp's gates during the war. Many important nonmilitary visitors spent time at the camp. Entertainers regaled the troops with shows, ranging from the simple to the elaborate. The list of entertainers was very long, including comedians Red Skelton and Bob Hope, and actresses Hedy Lamarr and Joan Blondell. The entertainers often brought their shows or USO camp shows to the large camp field house stage. Groups, such as the local rotary or the Oil Workers International Union, would visit the camp to see how their efforts to support the war were being realized. Visitors were always welcome, and many were given special accommodation. Some lucky International Oil Workers union members actually got to spend the night in the barracks and participate in actual tank destroyer training. That overnight opportunity surely generated many a hair-raising story for the workers to take back home. Some of the soldiers training at the camp were famous on their own merit, such as Louie L'Amour and Jackie Robinson. The civilian population around the camp grew enormously. Entire towns were built by the National Housing Authority to accommodate the workers supporting the post. The cooperative interaction between the civilian community and the Army was a key factor in the early success of Camp Hood.

As the German army was being squeezed on the eastern and western fronts, it was readily apparent that new tank destroyer battalions would not be needed. The German and Russian armor tactics evolved into a more integrated, organic approach. The German tanks were more dispersed by the end of the war, contained in massed formations. The massive German tank divisions were never again used as they had been when rolling through Poland and France. This dispersal was contrary to basic tank destroyer doctrine; by October 1943, tank destroyer training was being scaled back. By the end of 1943, 106 tank destroyer battalions were active; 61 battalions made it to Europe, and 10 went to the Pacific. The Unit Training Center had, in less than two years, trained 2 brigades, 21 groups, 100 battalions, and 1 separate company. In 18 months, 85,000 to 87,000 troops had passed through the center. The center took ill-equipped and undermanned units and shipped them out as well-trained combat teams. In 1944, the War Department announced its plan to merge the Tank Destroyer Officer Candidate School program with the Armored Command OCS at Fort Knox. The training activities at Camp Hood were placed directly under the authority of the Army Ground Forces' Replacement and School Command. The creation of new tank destroyer battalions ceased, and the Infantry Replacement Training Center became the primary occupant at Camp Hood.

In September 1945, Camp Hood became home to a separation camp to help process the many soldiers returning from the European theater. North Camp Hood was decommissioned at war's end, and it was decided to keep South Camp Hood in operation. This meant the Killeen and Gatesville area would be forever changed. Camp Hood became Fort Hood eight years after its official opening. Fort Hood would always have an armored component, and it would go on to become one of the largest active-duty posts in the United States.

# One

# THE CAMP

In December 1941, the War Department challenged the Army with developing a new concept of operations, focusing on antitank tactics. There was general concern, as few Army officers tasked with antitank defense had ever seen a real tank in action. A War Department memo on November 27, 1941, ordered the creation of the initial Tank Destroyer Tactical and Firing Center, which was to be located at Fort Meade, Maryland. The tank destroyer program was under the umbrella of Army Ground Forces Command, led by Gen. Leslie McNair. The inadequacies of the training base in Maryland were quickly realized by Army leaders. The soldiers needed to learn how to maneuver tank destroyer vehicles in difficult terrain and under various conditions. Large training grounds were needed for long-range firing, and Texas provided the ideal locale. On January 14, 1942, barely one month after the attack on Pearl Harbor, Killeen, Texas, was announced by Gen. Andrew D. Bruce as the location of the new tank destroyer training center. By April 2, the 893rd Tank Destroyer Battalion arrived at Killeen from Fort Meade, and Camp Hood was officially opened on September 18. Several hundred families had to sacrifice their properties and move from their homes in the communities of Clear Creek, Elijah, Sugarloaf, and Antelope to allow the Army to obtain the necessary 108,000 acres. Despite this hardship, a strong bond was developed between the Army and the local population. The local economy realized an unprecedented boom as soldiers poured into the camp for training. Undersecretary of War R.P. Patterson stated at the camp's opening ceremonies that the only way to save America was expressed in the Tank Destroyer Center's slogan, "Seek, Strike, Destroy." In only eight months, one of the most important combat training centers in the United States had been created.

Gen. Andrew D. Bruce, graduate of Texas A&M University, was the first Tank Destroyer Center commanding general. Bruce, at the rank of colonel, had initially been tasked with the chairing of the board to create and develop tank destroyer doctrine. He was then promoted to brigadier general and took over guiding the original tank destroyer doctrine and weapons development while at Camp Hood. Bruce was commanding general at Camp Hood from December 1, 1941, to May 25, 1943, when he was replaced by Gen. Orlando Ward. Bruce was instrumental in introducing many new and effective methods of training and instruction at the camp, and many of these were later adopted by the entire Army. He was awarded both the Army and Navy Distinguished Service Medals and the Air Medal. Bruce went on to become the president and, later, chancellor of the University of Houston.

The large garrison flag, measuring 20 feet by 38 feet, is being raised during the opening ceremonies for Camp Hood on September 18, 1942. The camp opened a mere 120 days after the start of construction. The grounds seen here are still in fairly primitive shape, with only crushed-stone roads and freshly turned earth. The camp's newly built chapel stands in the background.

Col. Charles M. Thirlkeld was Camp Hood's first post commander. He led the camp until January 1944. He was the executive officer under Gen. A.D. Bruce until July 21, 1942, when Bruce requested that Thirlkeld be appointed post commander. Thirlkeld entered the Army in 1920 and was an artillery officer by trade. He participated in developing and supporting the growth of the Tank Destroyer Center.

On behalf of those of us in the Army Service Forces whose duty and obligation it is, to provide the necessary services and supply for our armed forces in training and combat, I wish to express sincere appreciation for the wholehearted effort of all who have made possible the early completion of this camp.

As Camp Commander, I pledge the best use of these facilities, and assure you of the complete cooperation of the Army Service Forces in accomplishing its primary mission at Camp Hood-- that of providing all possible aid in the training of troops for the victory which must be ours.

This personal note was used for reference by Col. Charles M. Thirlkeld, the camp commander, for his portion of the official opening ceremonies for Camp Hood on September 18, 1942. Thirlkeld was in charge of the Army Service Forces personnel stationed at the camp. They were responsible for running and maintaining many of the camp's services and infrastructure.

The Camp Hood main entrance sign proudly displays the tank destroyer motto, with the insignia centered in the middle of the disk. The sign was erected around 1942. The motto, "Seek, Strike, Destroy," summarized the tank destroyer doctrine of aggressiveness. The insignia depicts a fierce black panther crushing an enemy tank in its jaws.

On January 30, 1942, Confederate army general John Bell Hood was announced as the namesake of Camp Hood. The name held historical significance in Texas. Hood, 33, was the youngest general in the Civil War to lead an independent army. Known for his fearlessness and aggressiveness, Hood was in charge of what was known as the Texas Brigade.

The terrain near Killeen, Texas, attracted the attention of the camp planners. The variety of hills, fields, and forested areas allowed for the simulation of a multitude of battlefield conditions. Large open spaces were needed to enable the firing of high-caliber guns mounted on the tank destroyers.

In 1942, War Highway 1 was claimed to be the shortest highway in Texas, at 819 feet in length. The entrance road to Camp Hood was given this honorary name by the Texas Highway Department, which constructed it. This honor was repeated at primary roads near several other military bases in Texas. Each base had its own numbered highway. Fort Bliss, for example, had Texas War Highway 11. Appropriately, a black plume of smoke from an Army training exercise or maneuver can be seen rising in the background of this photograph.

In these photographs, the school regiment passes in review on April 22, 1943. Traditionally, this is considered a dismounted parade, as the soldiers are on foot, as opposed to riding in their tank destroyer vehicles. Positioned next to the chapel is an M3 tank destroyer, which by the time of this parade was quickly becoming obsolete in the field. It was being replaced by the M10 tank destroyer.

This wood-frame building is the post headquarters, located on aptly named Headquarters Avenue, next to the finance office (left). These two buildings are a good example of the "temporary" buildings quickly erected as the base grew. They were simple structures with minimal finish work on the interior. These buildings were expected to last at least five years. The headquarters was one of the larger structures at the camp.

In February 1944, the novelty of freshly fallen snow appears at Camp Hood. It was the first snowfall in the area in decades. Of course, life went on in the camp as usual. The 50th Street Officers Club is shown in this wintry scene.

Camp Hood was lucky to have a professional painter in its midst, in the person of Sgt. Stanley Farnham. Here, Farnham is painting the mural on the east wall of the 162nd Street Service Club. Farnham also had his talent on display at the Eighth Army Service Force's Army Arts Exhibition at the Dallas Museum of Art from April 29 to May 13, 1945. Farnham attended Pratt Institute in New York. Prior to his Army career, he worked for the Lord & Thomas advertising agency, where he did illustrations for Lucky Strike and Frigidaire. These great murals were part of a series painted in the summer of 1943 in most of the clubs and common areas at Camp Hood.

This incredible mural was painted by Sergeant Farnham and Sgt. Arthur Bratton Jr. in the noncommissioned officers center. The highly detailed painting shows the evolution of the US Army from the Revolutionary War to World War II. Confederate army general John Hood is

depicted just over the left door. The original self-propelled M3 tank destroyer dominates the middle of the mural, over the double doors. The letters AGF stand for Army Ground Forces, one of a triad of branches of the Army representing ground combat forces.

21

The newly constructed post chapel is seen here around 1942. This is one of several churches and places of worship at the camp. The simple design easily conveys the function of the building. According to the *Hood Panther*, services were held for Protestant nondenominational, Jewish, Episcopalian, Lutheran, Roman Catholic, and Latter-day Saints adherents. Services were held at 10 different locations throughout the camp.

At the camp post office in December 1943, workers sort through a pile of incoming Christmas packages. Mail volume tripled during the holiday season. Civilian and military personnel worked side by side in the post office. Civilians heavily augmented many of the service duties at the camp. The population of Killeen grew from approximately 1,200 people to 30,000 to provide support to the camp as it grew in the spring of 1942.

This is a rear view of the very large, new post office around 1943. Direct access to a railroad spur greatly facilitated the movement of the copious quantities of letters and packages.

The central bus station is pictured here around 1943. This station was built to facilitate the great demand placed on the two local bus services to ferry soldiers and workers to and from area towns and to and from McClosky General Hospital. The local bus services created friction with African American soldiers, who were made to sit at the rear of the bus, as was the custom at that time in the area. Many officers allowed African American troops the use of camp trucks in an effort to alleviate tensions generated by the bus service.

An M10 tank destroyer with a three-inch gun motor carriage rests on a flatbed railroad car at the Camp Hood terminus. The M10, introduced in 1942, was the first true purpose-built American tank hunter. The M10 was armed with a three-inch antitank gun and the chassis from the M4A3 tank. Between 1942 and 1943, 6,706 M10 models were built. The most decorated American soldier, Audie Murphy, earned his Medal of Honor at the Battle of the Colmar Pocket using the heavy machine gun of an abandoned and burning M10 to hold off a company of German infantry.

This is the famous "deuce and a half," or "deuce" truck, a Diamond T Model 968. This one was named "Hercules" by its operator at the Camp Hood rail yard around 1943. This truck was the workhorse of the US military in World War II, the first war in which the production of massive numbers of trucks completely changed the tactics of warfare. The US automotive industry poured out hundreds of thousands of jeeps, trucks, and armored vehicles.

Resting on railcars at the Camp Hood yard are three Dodge WC-57 command cars and two Willys MB jeeps. The Marmon-Herrington was considered the grandfather of the jeep. The well-known jeep model was originally designed by Roy Evans and called the "Blitz Buggy." The Willys Overland Company eventually won the contract to build the jeep, due to its superior Go Devil engine. Many hundreds of thousands of jeeps would be built for the war. An important component of the training at the Tank Destroyer Center was the loading and unloading of equipment on train cars.

In the above photograph, an unknown civilian editor (left) and the Army newspaper editor, T.Sgt. Ivan Smith, work on the official camp newspaper, the *Hood Panther*. Smith edited the paper from its beginning until February 1944. The first issue was published on December 10, 1942. It was published bimonthly until July 1943, and then weekly until June 1944. Shown below is the masthead of the *Hood Panther*. The paper was created to help boost morale and keep soldiers informed of the happenings around the camp and in the nearby towns.

The camp field house is pictured in 1943. It was located on Headquarters Avenue, near the camp entrance road, Hood Road. This was the largest entertainment venue at Camp Hood, with seating for approximately 5,000. Well-known acts such as Bob Hope and Red Skelton would appear at the field house.

Maj. Gen. Orlando Ward was the second commanding general of Camp Hood, serving from May 26, 1943, to October 24, 1943. Ward brought his recent combat experience against the German Afrika Korps in Tunisia to Camp Hood's training grounds, emphasizing individual soldier drills and meticulous small-unit training. In his effort to stress the effects of terrain on the flow of battle, Ward had new terrain plots created, used to demonstrate the change of visibility and to allow planning and visualization of battlefield conditions. Intelligent aggression was also emphasized, along with the complex coordination of all units involved in the field of battle.

Maj. Gen. John H. Hester was the third commanding general of Camp Hood, serving from October 24, 1943, to June 26, 1944. Hester continued the training policies of his predecessor while stressing gunner training and teamwork. Hester emphasized having the officers really know and understand the men under their command. He was soon confronted with the curtailment of demand for tank destroyer forces and the realignment of the camp's organization.

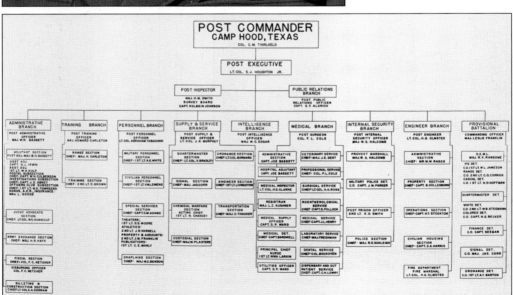

This chart depicts the Army Service Forces organization at Camp Hood. The many branches under the service force umbrella spanned all the crucial needs of the camp and its personnel.

A soldier uses an acetylene torch to cut off a damaged or weakened tie point on a piece of heavy equipment in the Camp Hood fabrication shop around 1943. The physical effects of realistic combat training and testing of experimental equipment required a well-equipped repair department.

This state-of-the-art bakery, one of several in the camp, features automated equipment. The bakeries had to feed the thousands of troops at Camp Hood. Up to 10,000 loaves of bread were baked daily at the camp. During World War II, many of the service functions in the Army, such as food preparation and laundry, were conducted by African American soldiers.

This photograph, taken by a Camp Hood signal corps photographer, shows Pvt. Marshal DeMuynck. The slogan reflects a common theme used by the Office of War Information, similar to "Loose Lips Sink Ships." The idea was handled uniquely by Pvt. Ivan Smith, the editor of the *Hood Panther*, where this photograph appeared. Smith placed signs under and over the mirrors in camp washrooms to help drive home the message that the life being saved could be one's own. This concept caught on and quickly spread across the camp. Many other military bases around the country also adopted this idea.

This photograph of an unknown wounded man gazing at a war bonds poster about sacrifice shows the commitment of US troops in the war. The soldier who volunteered for this photograph was most likely recovering from his injuries at McClosky General Army Hospital in Temple, Texas. The hospital specialized in amputations.

In this promotional photograph, taken in November 1943, Mardell Huseby, a civilian employee in the camp mess supervisors' office, places a suggestion in the "Ideas for Victory" box at Camp Hood. Civilians could receive a cash award from the War Department for ideas that provided a measurable savings toward the war effort. Awards ranged from $5 to $250. This was one of the many ways civilians could contribute to the war effort. Others included buying war bonds, planting Victory Gardens, rationing, and participating in collection drives to round up materials such as rubber for wartime production.

Col. James A. Bethea's wife is shown pinning brigadier general stars on the shoulders of his tunic. Bethea was the medical officer in charge of McClosky General Hospital in nearby Temple, Texas. When Bethea arrived in Temple, he was the only person assigned to the hospital. In 1942, 216 acres of land were purchased on the south side of Temple; 54 buildings were constructed in seven short months to create the large complex. The hospital, which quickly grew to 1,500 beds, was one of the largest general hospitals in the Army during the war. The specialty at McClosky was amputations. By the end of the war, the complex had grown to 190 buildings and included a nine-hole golf course, a pool, and tennis and handball courts. McClosky closed on December 31, 1946, and later became a Veterans Administration hospital.

This is an early artist's concept of the famed tank destroyer emblem, modified for placement on the post commander's desk or as a vehicle badge. The same design was used for the tank destroyer shoulder patch, but with the "Seek, Strike, Destroy" motto removed for simplicity.

A Good Conduct Medal is presented to M.Sgt. Valeria Henderson (right) of the Army Service Force. He was commander of the 3rd Automotive and Tank Platoon. The post commander, Col. Charles M. Thirlkeld, is doing the honors. Henderson had 21 years of service at the time of the award.

Above, freshly trained tank destroyer personnel board a troop train, most likely for their next stint in field maneuvers before heading overseas. Troop trains were used to ferry vast numbers of military personnel around the country. Many of the trains included sleepers and full meal service, depending on the length of the trip. With the ability of overnight travel, troop movements could be scheduled much more efficiently. Between December 1941 and June 1945, railroads carried approximately 44 million members of the military around the continental United States. Pictured below is a Pullman car bearing the name *Killarney Rose*. A total of 2,400 Pullman sleepers were built specifically for the war effort.

TANK DESTROYER CENTER
CAMP HOOD, TEXAS

*Sunday 5:15*
*Aug 8, 1943*

Among the more popular items in the camp post exchange was the unique stationery, such as that shown here, used to send letters home. This stationery depicts the gunnery skills of the tank destroyer men. It also captures the interesting terrain of bluffs and fields located within the base.

PORTION OF NAZI VILLAGE USED IN TEACHING VILLAGE FIGHTING, CAMP HOOD, TEXAS

Among the many innovative training ideas used at Camp Hood was a life-sized village for developing urban fighting skills. The Nazi Village came complete with a Gestapo headquarters. The village's main street is seen here in a World War II–era postcard produced by Barton Publishing.

The above photograph of a meeting of the minds was taken at Fort Sam Houston, Texas, during one of many organizational meetings held in June 1942 to determine the operations of Camp Hood. In the first row, second from left, is the post commander, Col. Charles M. Thirlkeld. Shown below is Special Order No. 141, requesting attendance at the event. The meeting drew officers from the infantry, cavalry, military police, field artillery, and the corps of engineers.

HEADQUARTERS EIGHTH CORPS AREA

SPECIAL ORDERS,                                        Fort Sam Houston, Texas,
                                                                   May 25, 1942.
NO.        141.                    - E X T R A C T -

              x                         x                         x

        32.  Each of the following named O will proceed from his proper sta,
as  indicated after his name, to Hq 8CA, Ft Sam Houston, Tex, at such time
as will enable him to report not later than 8:30 AM, June 2, 1942, to the
CA Comdr, for temp duty at this Hq:

COL HENRY A. FINCH, 02119, CE, CASC, Camp Barkeley, Tex;
COL EDGAR W. TAULBEE, 02834, Cav, CASC, Ft Bliss, Tex;
COL FRANK E. BONNEY, 03641, Inf, CASC, Camp Bowie, Tex;
COL KENNETH S. PERKINS, 02446, FA, CASC, Ft Sill, Okla;
COL EARL C. FLEGEL, 06800, MP, CASC, Camp Wolters, Tex;
COL LANDON J. LOCKETT, 011107, Inf, CASC, Camp Chaffee, Ark;
COL HENRY McE. PENDLETON, 03829, Cav, CASC, Camp Claiborne, La;
COL CHARLES M. THIRLKELD, 09057, FA, CASC, Camp Hood, Temple, Tex;
LT COL CLAIR F. SCHUMACHER, 0176631, Inf, CASC, Camp Joseph T. Robinson, Ark;
LT COL JOHN P. WHEELER, 03494, Cav, CASC, Camp Wallace, Tex;
LT COL GROVER C. GRAHAM, 06034, Inf, CASC, Camp Joseph T. Robinson, Ark;
LT COL KENNETH F. HANST, 05124, Inf, CASC, Camp Beauregard, La;
LT COL OTTO WAGNER, 03466, Cav, CASC, Camp Polk, La;
LT COL PEYTON C. WINLOCK, 08074, FA, CASC, Camp Beauregard, La.

Shown here are two Camp Hood military police (MP) officers and their canine helpers. Any sizable military base has a law-enforcement presence. The MPs fell under the Army Service Force. It was noted in the *Hood Panther* that the dogs were very successful in guarding the camp's water wells.

Maj. C.F. Aldrich, the camp adjutant, is seen here around 1943. The adjutant would assist the senior officer in executing his duties and fell under the administrative branch. The adjutant was directly responsible for the postal, investigative, officers club, and war bonds subsections.

Soldiers stand at attention as the inspection of a Tank Destroyer School truck battalion ensues. As in any military inspection, everything has its place and must be neat as a pin. The battalion is being inspected by Col. Lansing McVickar, commanding officer of the training brigade. This African American battalion served at Camp Hood to help facilitate the training of newly formed tank destroyer battalions stationed temporarily at the camp. In one week, the truck battalion's vehicles would log approximately 48,000 miles and haul 36,903 men to various points around the camp. The unit comprised 440 vehicles, including trucks, jeeps, and half-tracks.

Lt. Frank W. Mayborn joined the Army in 1942 at age 36 and served as a public-relations officer at Camp Hood. He was influential as a civilian and soldier at the camp and in the Temple area. Mayborn retired as a major and was awarded a Bronze Star for his service. A well-known newspaper publisher and philanthropist, he played a large role in Bell County, Texas. His personal contributions as a civilian and soldier to the Fort Hood community over several decades were so substantial that the fort's east gate was named in his honor. Mayborn was on the Fort Hood Civilian Advisory Board from its establishment in 1963 until his death in 1987.

Col. Charles M. Thirlkeld (left) confers over a document with an unknown major around the summer of 1943.

Col. Charles M. Thirlkeld (left), Camp Hood post commander, stands next to Col. Joseph Franklin Battley, executive for the Service Commands Office Chief of Administrative Services. Battley would later become a brigadier general. This photograph was taken around 1943.

This is a group photograph of the camp's Service Force officers around 1943. Col. Charles M. Thirlkeld is at center in the first row.

One of the official tank destroyer bands is seen in front of the headquarters building, ready for a parade. The signature orange and black bass drum is right of center. There were multiple bands at the camp, at least two for parades. Many tank destroyer battalions formed their own bands during their time at the camp.

Colors pass in review, going down Headquarters Avenue around 1943. This is a dismounted parade. In the background, an M3 type tank destroyer is being used as a review stand. This was common in the regular parades, held several times a week at the camp.

This photograph of the Camp Hood countryside is unusual in that it used infrared film, evidenced by the white glow of the normally green leaves. The photograph was probably taken in the spring of 1943. Leaves reflect the most infrared radiation in the spring. This type of film, being very difficult to manage, may have been used for experimental purposes at the camp.

These photographs show the Texas countryside within the Camp Hood training grounds around 1944. Seen below are the steep hills, streams, stands of trees, and rolling prairies that carpet the countryside. The above photograph displays the excellent variety of rough terrain available at Camp Hood for training purposes, including the Blackwell Mountains. The mountains served to break up the view and helped to emphasize targeting sight lines and illustrate how visibility can change rapidly during combat. This was a point of emphasis for Gen. Hester after he returned from fighting the Germans in North Africa. When Hester assumed command of Camp Hood, he had small-scale terrain models built in each training unit to allow the demonstration of visibility concepts.

Maj. Gen. Richard Donovan (left) and Col. Charles Thirlkeld inspect the camp in February 1943. Thirlkeld was in command of the 1848 Service Unit at Camp Hood. Donovan was the commanding general of the 8th Service Command of the Army Service Forces from 1940 to 1945. The 8th Service Command was headquartered in Dallas and covered the region including Arkansas, Texas, Louisiana, New Mexico, and Oklahoma. The Army Service Forces was one of the three autonomous components of the Army during World War II. The many disparate and unrelated missions of the units of the service command made it very unwieldy to organize and control. With the issuance of a new War Department organization, the Army Service Forces was officially disbanded on June 11, 1946.

Shown above are officers of the Army Service Forces stationed at Camp Hood. Mounted around the upper railing of the room are the heraldry of the different tank destroyer battalions. The officers are identified by number and listed below. The titles describing the areas of responsibility of the officers illustrate the broad scope of the newly created branch called the Army Service Forces. Any responsibility not covered by the Army Ground Forces or the Army Air Forces fell under the Army Service Forces. With no organic or historical governance in place, this created a very diverse and inherently unwieldy force. Shortly after the end of the war, the Army Service Forces was disbanded.

1. LT. COL. E. A. DUNNAH
   Battalion Company Officer
   Replacement Training Center

2. COL. F. L. COLE
   Camp Surgeon

3. CAPT. G. C. BEAKLEY
   Purchasing Branch Supply

4. LT. D. A. LOWE
   Assistant Post Engineer

5. LT. COL. O. A. ACRES
   Camp Executive Officer

6. LT. A. J. SILFEN
   Chemical Warfare

7. MAJ. H. G. BECKER
   Assistant Inspecting General

8. MAJ. R. H. BOAS
   Camp Engineer

9. MAJ. T. H. TALBOT
   Camp Chaplain

10. MAJ. L. FRANKLIN
    Commanding Officer Provisional Bn.

11. 1ST. LT. T. F. JORDON
    Fiscal & Audit Branch

12. LT. COL. PAUL JONES
    Director Fiscal Division

13. MAJ. H. CARLTON
    Assistant Range Officer
    Tank Destroyer Center

14. LT. COL. H. M. SMITH
    Camp Inspector General

15. LT. COL. J. P. CAULK
    Maintenance Branch

16. CAPT. W. S. TOWNSEND
    Camp Safety Officer

17. COL. C. M. THIRLKELD
    Camp Commander

18. MAJ. C. C. THACKER
    Camp Transportation Officer

19. COL. D. R. DUNKLE
    Camp Executive Officer
    North Camp Hood

20. MAJ. R. F. LUSH
    Camp Ordnance Officer

21. MAJ. C. F. ALDRICH
    Camp Adjutant

22. CAPT. W. H. YANCEY
    Camp Billeting Officer

23. LT. COL. K. S. WHITE
    Security & Intelligence Div.
    Provost Marshal

24. LT. COL. H. M. CARROLL
    Personnel Division

25. CAPT. W. R. LACE
    Transportation Adv. Comm

26. MAJ. H. R. HAYES
    Camp Executive Officer

27. MAJ. W. C. EDGAR
    Intelligence Officer

28. MAJ. F. M. PARKER
    Camp Training Officer

29. LT. J. FRANKLIN
    Special Service

30. LT. COL. C. H. BOOTH, JR.
    Camp Public Relations
    Officer

31. CAPT. JOHN H. MORRIS
    War Bond Officer
    Army Emergency Relief

Shown here are examples of the heraldry of the tank destroyer battalions. These symbols were not official at the time, as the approval of heraldry was halted during World War II. They are, from left to right, (top row) 889th, 816th, 645th, and 601st; (second row) 828th, 646th, 631st, and 795th; (third row) 827th, 705th, 773rd, and 813th; (bottom row) 822nd, 628th, 643rd, and 637th. At Camp Hood, 100 tank destroyer battalions were trained for combat.

The sun sets on an M3 tank destroyer at Camp Hood. The M3 served its purpose as one of the original expedient weapons that allowed the tank destroyer program to proceed at a timely pace and start actual training without a true tank killer weapon. The M3 was short-lived as a tank destroyer, quickly replaced by the much more effective and capable M10 and then the M18. The M3 held a special place in the hearts of the battalions, and its image was often used to represent the tank destroyers.

# *Two*

# THE TRAINING

Camp Hood was the nexus of all tank destroyer activity. The center was responsible for the training of individuals, the activation of units, and the development of doctrine and equipment. The primary components of the center were the Unit Training Center, which organized and trained new battalions, the Individual Training Center, and the Replacement Training Center. There also came into being an Officer Candidate School. The training at Camp Hood emphasized an intelligent aggressiveness and a courageous spirit. The tank destroyer man was to have a sense of élan and spirit. One of the primary goals of training was to erase any fear of armored forces. What would today be considered special operations, such as raiding a tank park and using improvised weapons or small arms to destroy tanks, was considered "close combat" in the tank destroyer world.

Many innovative training methods were developed at Camp Hood, such as battle conditioning, infiltration, woods fighting, subcaliber firing, and village fighting. Unique features on the different training courses included pop-up targets, traps, live-firing machine guns, first-rate conventional gunnery ranges, and underground, darkened tunnels used as firing ranges. Many of these advanced methods were borrowed from British commando training. As word spread, many of these training techniques were taken up at other Army training camps. Several new, complicated concepts were used in overall tank destroyer training, including radio communications, advanced reconnaissance using motorcycles, road priorities, and, most important, multiple unit coordination. It was expected that 19 weeks would be needed to complete training: 6 weeks for basic training, and 13 weeks of technical and tactical training. The basic component ensured that soldiers were experienced in the many small arms needed and that they had a prescribed level of expertise to advance to tactical training. The basic-training school also ensured that units were complete and fully manned. Tactical training focused on the coordinated action of the squad, section, platoon, company, and battalion. In less than two years, 2 brigades, 21 groups, 100 battalions, and 1 company were trained at the Tank Destroyer Center. The center contributed many good soldiers and developed new training methods for the Army.

Tank Destroyer Center commanding general Andrew D. Bruce (right) hands over operations to Gen. Orlando Ward in May 1943. Bruce went on to command the 77th Infantry Division through battles in Guam, Leyte, Ryukyu, and Le Shima in the Pacific theater. After the Japanese surrendered, Bruce served as the military governor of Hokkaido while his division occupied the island. He went on to command the 7th Infantry Division in Korea. Bruce retired from the Army as a lieutenant general on July 31, 1954. He also served as the president of the Houston Chamber of Commerce. The Bruce Memorial Hall housing complex at Fort Hood is named after him.

Lt. Gen. John H. Hester was the third commanding general at Camp Hood, serving from October 24, 1943, to June 26, 1944. He brought considerable combat experience with him. Hester commanded the 43rd Infantry Division, which conducted landings on the Russell and New Georgia Islands in the Solomon Islands. Because of ill health, Hester was sent stateside, where he took command of the Tank Destroyer School. Hester always stressed the importance of leaders thoroughly knowing their equipment and their men. He also stressed, as was the tradition of the tank destroyers, the need for accuracy in firing their weapons and teamwork. Hester was faced with reorganizing the camp's mission, as the need declined for the training of new tank destroyer battalions. The end of the war was looming as the German army began to fade.

Chief of Staff George Marshall had the daunting task of creating a modern army, 40 times the size of the prewar US Army. One of his mandates to Gen. Leslie McNair was to develop antitank weapons and to create a new antitank force and doctrine. This was the birth of the tank destroyers.

Gen. George Patton, shown here on the right at the Malta Conference, was a vocal critic of tank destroyer doctrine. Patton felt that an army should fight tanks with tanks. His viewpoint would eventually come to fruition, as the tank destroyer doctrine was never fully adopted on the battlefield. There are many reasons that the doctrine did not succeed, but the tank destroyer training center produced highly desired soldiers known for their first-shot accuracy and esprit de corps.

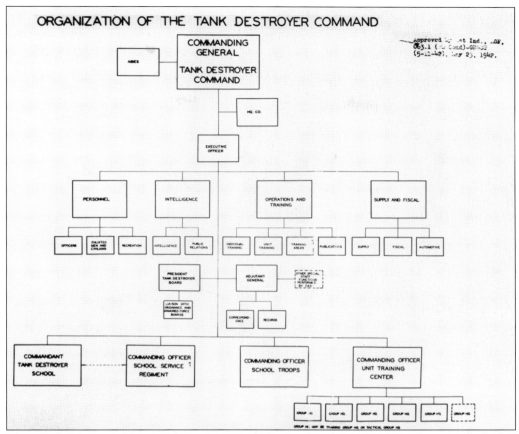

ORGANIZATION OF THE TANK DESTROYER COMMAND

This Tank Destroyer Command organizational chart is dated May 11, 1942, four months before the official opening of Camp Hood. One of the many difficulties during the early days of the camp was finding qualified personnel. Many of the officers and men needed to staff the training center had little or no experience in antitank combat.

The headquarters of the Tank Destroyer Training Center is shown around 1943. This was the hub of all aspects of training in the early days of Camp Hood. Tank destroyer doctrine and the testing and evaluating of new vehicles and weapons were also coordinated here. Eventually, several different training functions would begin to replace or supplant the tank destroyer training at Camp Hood.

Shown at left is the original tank destroyer patch, depicting a black panther against an orange background, crushing a tank in its jaws. Designed by Gen. Andrew Bruce and his staff, this original design has eight bogie wheels. To many, the tank being crushed looked like an American tank, so the patch was changed to show only four bogie wheels (below). It is rumored that the original eight-wheel design was too hard on the embroidery needles that produced the patches and, hence, needed to be simplified.

# TD Insignia

Our insignia is an emblem of a panther
Who crushes a tank and breaks it in two.
Its background is orange with a border of black,
And the black face within is quick to attack.
Lips, nose and eyebrows are of reddish hue,
With white eyes and whiskers, it's teeth are two.
Red means danger, black means death,
White brings out its ferocious sight,
 The huns in Africa know I'm right.
It's the Tank Destroyer* emblem. the Army's joy,
And its slogan is. "Seek, Strike, Destroy!"
—Pvt. Bernard Weiser
812th TD Bn., Co. C.

A poem published in the *Hood Panther*, written by Pvt. Bernard Weiser in July 1943, describes the tank destroyer insignia. The panther patch was a point of pride for the soldiers and was unique to battalion-strength units.

Some tank destroyer battalions designed shoulder patches of their own. Generally, these patches were not authorized for wear, but they ended up on uniforms anyway. This patch was worn by the soldiers of the 802nd Tank Destroyer Battalion.

A towed antitank gun is set up for action. These units would deploy quickly, fire, and then move. This was not the usual technique for artillery, which was usually set up behind the front lines and remained stationary. This type of tank destroyer unit was very mobile and could be set up in various conditions.

An M4 medium Sherman tank pulverizes obstacles at Camp Hood. This tank was an improvement on the M3 tank, with thicker armor and a more powerful 75-millimeter gun mounted on the turret. The Sherman was a good match for the German Panzer II and Panzer III tanks, but it was severely outgunned by the larger guns and heavier armor on the newer Panther and Tiger tanks.

An M3 light tank catches a little air on the Camp Hood fields around 1942. These tanks were used as moving targets for training at Camp Hood. Many antitank officers had never seen a real tank in action. This tank was used in the Lend-Lease program by British and Commonwealth forces. The M3, nicknamed "Honey" for its smooth, fast ride, was the first American-crewed tank to engage the enemy in World War II. The small, 37-millimeter gun and thin armor was an issue against German tanks. Many of the light M3s were used for scouting and infantry support purposes as the war wore on. The light M3 proved useful against the smaller Japanese tanks on the islands and in the jungles of the Pacific.

These photographs show a nighttime firing demonstration of the 50-caliber machine gun. The glowing lines are tracer bullets, placed at intervals of every fifth bullet in the belt of ammunition feeding into the weapon. Night fire exercises were a standard part of tank destroyer training. Some small-arms training was even conducted in a darkened tunnel constructed for the purpose of teaching shooting by hearing.

In the above photograph, towed antitank units practice camouflage techniques on the edge of a firing range. The M3 half-tracks were used to tow the guns. The vehicles are lined up just below the firing range. The below photograph is a close-up of a camouflaged M5 three-inch towed gun. This is the same gun used by the famous 614th Tank Destroyer Battalion, one of the few African American combat units formed in World War II.

This portion of the obstacle course immediately followed the water-hazard river crossing section. This was used in the advanced training school. Basic training was introduced at Camp Hood to prepare soldiers for more advanced, specialized combat training. The Basic Unit Training School headquarters was located at North Camp Hood. This unit was later named the Individual Unit Training School.

A near hit! An M10 traverses a field during combat simulation. Such field training was the order of the day at Camp Hood. The first true tank destroyer weapon was developed from the chassis of the Sherman tank, with an open turret to provide better visibility in action.

58

Shown above is the live fire portion of the infiltration course at Camp Hood. Live machine-gun fire was used; a machine gunner fired 24 inches over the heads of the men crawling 120 yards on their stomachs under the barbed wire. Explosions were also simulated to create shock, smoke, and confusion. The breadth of the live-fire portion of the course can be seen below. At far left, men watch their fellow soldiers struggle along.

Pictured above is the end of the infiltration course. This was part of the advanced training portion of the tank destroyer school. The soldiers are shown making their last dash to the protection of the ditch and embankment, for a respite from all the hectic action in the live-fire field. This course, the first live-fire combat training devised by the Army for World War II, was quickly imitated at other Army bases. Below, the weary soldiers pull themselves up and out of the safety of the ditch. Now, they can watch and yell support to the next group of soldiers coming through.

Time to hustle off to the next phase of training. The men of the Tank Destroyer School and the Infantry Replacement Training Center were always on the move. As training progressed, 16-mile and 25-mile hikes with full packs were not uncommon.

An M10 tank destroyer heads over the dirt roads of Camp Hood. Mobility was very important in the tank destroyer doctrine. The M10 could reach 32 miles per hour on a paved road. Move and shoot was the order of the day. M10s were not designed for head-to-head fighting with tank groups; instead, they were designed to shoot and then move.

Here, soldiers load an M1 bazooka with an M6A1 rocket. The electric igniter wire can be seen in the tail, by the rocket fins. An electric charge went from a battery, through the wire, to the rocket motor. Tank destroyer soldiers were among the first trained in the use of the bazooka. Many bazookas were distributed in North Africa with little or no training; they were considered generally ineffective against tanks unless used at close range.

Smoke, explosions, and gunfire mark the beginning of the infiltration course. As seen here, the going is tough and dangerous as the soldiers try to keep their bearings and head for the sound of machine-gun fire. This was one of the innovative training methods developed at Camp Hood.

This soldier is ignoring the Texas mud in his foxhole and carefully aiming his Enfield rifle. Tank destroyer basic unit training included small arms, such as the M1917 Enfield rifle. This rifle was the main weapon used by the American Expeditionary Force in World War I. This soldier was demonstrating for a *March of Time* radio serial crew recording at Camp Hood in September 1942. This rifle was primarily used for training purposes or by artillerymen early in World War II. The M1 Garand quickly replaced the M1917 during the war. This soldier has two practice dummy grenades at the ready. Basic unit training was very important in ensuring that the individual soldier had the proper skills for the advanced unit training portion of tank destroyer school. It was initially noticed that incoming soldiers were ill prepared for the advanced school, especially in small-arms proficiency.

The sprawling north cantonment is seen here around 1943. Training camps during the war were very barracks-intensive. The volume of soldiers receiving training grew rapidly as the war intensified in Europe and the Pacific. The soldiers' quarters are on the right side of the main road running through the middle of the camp. The motor pools and heavy equipment were positioned in the areas on the left side of the main road.

A mile-long convoy winds along a back country road as the tank destroyers deploy through the environs of Camp Hood. Fast movement and highly coordinated communications, new concepts to warfare training, were greatly stressed and constantly practiced in tank destroyer training at Camp Hood.

The tank destroyer soldiers proved themselves worthy. Here, S.Sgt. Harry Zitkovitch (right) of Hartford, Connecticut, receives the Bronze Star from Maj. Gen. Robert W. Grow, the commanding general of the 6th Armored Division, Third Army, at a ceremony near Boevanoe, Luxembourg. Zitkovitch received the award for meritorious achievement while fighting on the Siegfried Line, also known as "The Dragon's Teeth." The Siegfried Line was a static defense system similar to the Maginot Line. This photograph, dated January 30, 1945, was taken by Army Signal Corps photographer Pfc. Joseph Lapine.

The M3 tank destroyer is depicted in the postcard Camp Hood Story Series. This item, sold at the camp post exchange, was bought by soldiers to send back home. The series was published by Barton Publishing Company in 1943.

Against the Texas sky, a soldier loads the ammunition belt of a .30-06 machine gun located on the turret of an M3 Grant tank. Undoubtedly, the crew is preparing for exercises in the field. Older tanks approaching obsolescence were typically used for target practice. Small-caliber weapons were used to shoot at a buttoned-up tank. This was a training method developed at Camp Hood.

A T22 armored car, soon to be called the M8, also known as "the Greyhound," moves in the infamous Camp Hood mud hole around 1942. The armored cars were used for reconnaissance, due to their speed and mobility. They did not have the armor protection or firepower to engage a tank head-on with only a 37-millimeter gun. It looks like it is faring well in the mud and water.

This is an aerial view of the massive training grounds of Camp Hood around 1943. Various types of firing ranges can be seen in the foreground. Marksmanship was heavily stressed at the camp. Tank destroyer soldiers were well known for their accuracy. The use of subcaliber shooting originated at Camp Hood. This method allowed smaller weapons to be used to simulate large guns.

The dollhouse-scaled Nazi Village was an exact replica of the full-sized village standing nearby, used for what is now termed urban combat. This was one of the best examples of cutting-edge training methods developed at Camp Hood. The miniature village was used to provide a bird's-eye view to the trainees for planning purposes and instruction on combat schemes. Receiving fire from above was stressed in the village training. This instruction was also part of the Officer Candidate School training at the camp. There were pop-up targets and traps throughout the village. This method was used later at other Army training bases.

An M18 "Hellcat" gun motor carriage negotiates its way through the trees of Camp Hood. The M18 may be taking a position to fire at a target. It was training procedure to move to an advantageous position, fire, and then move on. This method of combat is the seek, strike, and destroy part of the tank destroyer doctrine. In July 1944, the 630th Tank Destroyer Battalion accounted for destroying 54 Panther medium tanks and Tiger 1 heavy tanks in battles, with only 17 M18s lost. As the German tank numbers started to dwindle, M18s started to see more use as mobile artillery. The M18, with a top speed of 55 to 60 miles per hour, was the fastest armored vehicle in the Army for many years, even after the war.

This is an air demonstration over Camp Hood by B26 Marauders. Strafing runs and close air support were demonstrated to allow the concept of air support to become familiar to the tank destroyer troops and officers.

The troop train was usually the first and last thing a soldier would see when arriving or leaving Camp Hood. As shown here, a good soldier always sleeps when given the opportunity. Since these soldiers have tank destroyer patches on their shoulders, they are probably off to their next training billet before heading overseas.

Shown here is the cover of the field manual for tank destroyer doctrine. The doctrine attained official status in the form of the War Department's FM 18-5, Tank Destroyer Field Manual, Organization and Tactics of Tank Destroyer Units. Work on FM 18-5 began in January 1942 at the Tank Destroyer Tactical and Firing Center. A prepublication draft was distributed to tank destroyer units on March 19. The official publication date was June 16, only six months after the writing began.

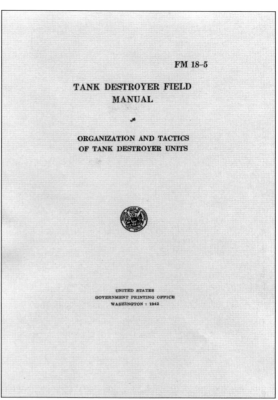

FM 18-5

TANK DESTROYER FIELD
MANUAL

ORGANIZATION AND TACTICS
OF TANK DESTROYER UNITS

UNITED STATES
GOVERNMENT PRINTING OFFICE
WASHINGTON : 1942

Shown here is the American Southwest version of a Nazi village. This small village provided experience in house-to-house and street fighting. It was called "village fighting" at the time of the training. This village came complete with a Gestapo headquarters at the end of the street.

An M10 gun motor carriage easily traverses a mud and water obstacle. Camp Hood was also a weapons-testing and trial center for tank destroyer weapons and vehicles. The mud hole was a test that all the vehicles had to go through.

The M3, the original tank destroyer motor carriage, was the first mobile antitank gun developed specifically for tank destroyer use. It was a weapon of expediency, as it was cobbled together from an armored personnel carrier and a French 75-millimeter gun. Some additional armor was placed around the gun to protect the gunners. The M3 was quickly replaced by the M10 tank destroyer, a superior weapon.

Above, the M10 tank destroyer, sometimes called the M10 gun motor carriage, sits in a field in Camp Hood. The M10 truly started the evolution of tank destroyers in the US Army, as the next several versions of tank destroyers would improve upon this model's capabilities. The next version (below) was the M18, which had the same main gun but was much faster. The M18 had the best kill-to-loss ratio of any American tank destroyer. It was the fastest US tank until the M1 Abrams was introduced. There was also an improved version of the M10, the M36, which had a powerful 90-millimeter gun in place of the 75-millimeter. The larger gun had success against the thick German armor.

WATER HAZARD,
TANK DESTROYER OBSTACLE COURSE

This is a very early training photograph of the water-hazard portion of the obstacle course at Camp Hood. Note the "doughboy," or M1917-type helmets worn by US soldiers until 1942. The doughboy helmets were quickly replaced by the M1 helmet, which was used until 1985. This image was part of the Camp Hood Story Series produced by Barton Publishing.

A group of heavily armed tank destroyer soldiers traverse a stream at the camp. These men appear to be carrying Thompson M1 submachine guns. Tank destroyer trainees were exposed to a larger variety of small arms than a typical infantryman would see. The noncommissioned officers are carrying the 1911 model .45-caliber pistol, standard issue for the time.

74

Members of the 614th Tank Destroyer Battalion load their three-inch gun. This unit started tank destroyer training with the M3 destroyer, but was reorganized as a towed-gun battalion. The 614th battalion distinguished itself in combat in the European theater. Its members accumulated an impressive list of awards for a unit of its size. The 3rd platoon from Company C, after taking heavy losses, with more than half its men injured or killed, was awarded four Silver Stars, nine Bronze Stars, and a Congressional Medal of Honor. It was the only African American unit to receive the Presidential Unit Citation during World War II. The unit performed occupation duties after the war in Germany until the battalion was disbanded on January 31, 1946, at Camp Kilmer, New Jersey. (Courtesy of the National Archives.)

Shown here is a tank destroyer pioneer platoon in training. The pioneers were specialists in constructing bridges, ramps, and whatever else it took to keep the battalion moving. They were also demolition experts, called in to remove obstacles in the way. The pioneers did not always have

the materials available to them as did a regular Army construction battalion. The pioneer platoons were skilled at finding what they needed and getting the job done with what was available.

An M3 Grant tank negotiates the chimneys of a ruined farmhouse on the Camp Hood training grounds. Light tanks and obsolete models of tanks were used for training purposes. It appears that the soldier at right is preparing to throw a sticky bomb or grenade at the tank. These tanks gave the antitank crews a good feel for shooting at moving targets. Despite this particular tank's obsolete design, it saw plenty of action in Africa.

This is one of the camp's small-arms firing ranges. The men practice adjusting the sights on their 1917 Enfield rifles. The Enfield rifle was used primarily for training in the United States. These rifles would soon be replaced with the M1 Garand rifle, the most commonly used rifle by the US Army in World War II.

Soldiers watch a demonstration of knot-tying. This skill was not just for sailors; it was especially important to the pioneer companies of the tank destroyers. The pioneers were invaluable as the builders and engineers of their tank destroyer battalions, responsible for constructing every conceivable device, including bridges, ramps, and shelters, and for destroying anything that impeded the movement of tank destroyers. Knot-tying skills also came in handy when lashing items to motor gun carriages. The knot board shown here was placed in the Tank Destroyer Museum and then donated at the end of the war to area Boy Scouts.

These soldiers, having graduated from Camp Hood, find themselves in a quiet spot while fighting in Europe. Their M10 provides a little shade and protection for a dice game. All of their belongings are strapped carefully to the vehicle. The M10 was their luggage carrier and home away from home at times. (Courtesy of the National Archives.)

Soldiers crawl in the Texas dirt and mud at Camp Hood. One holds a Thompson submachine gun, and the other has a knife. The Thompson gun was not normally used by infantry troops. Tank destroyer training stressed practice with all varieties of small arms. This type of training was similar to that of Army Rangers in World War II, or what is now called special operations.

The Tank Destroyer School taught a unique method of shooting pistols and rifles in combat situations, as shown here. This method was meant to give soldiers a means of aiming and firing without thought, using reflex. Soldiers were taught to keep their weapons level and pointed in the direction of their bodies. Using dark tunnels, they were also taught a means of aiming with their ears. This method produced surprisingly good results.

Soldiers relax with a dummy hand grenade in a muddy foxhole at Camp Hood. They were partaking in a demonstration for the *March of Time* radio serial just before the official opening of the camp in September 1942. *March of Time* serials kept citizens on the home front informed of the activities of the armed forces during the war. Radio and movie short subjects were used by *March of Time* to convey soldiers' stories.

Top brass inspects a T70 prototype gun motor carriage. This test vehicle would become the M18 Hellcat, the fastest armored vehicle in the US arsenal for many years. Gen. Leslie McNair (leaning on the front of the T70) and Gen. Orlando Ward (standing on top) look closely at the vehicle. All gun motor carriages went through rigorous testing at Camp Hood.

The rope-climbing portion of the obstacle course is pictured here. This was one of the strength- and confidence-building obstacles used to bring soldiers to an acceptable level for the advanced training courses. It was observed that many of the new trainees in the advanced program were not of the same initial level of ability. This photograph was part of the Camp Hood Story Series produced by Barton Publishing.

This is a front view of the original M3 tank destroyer. This vehicle was considered an expedient weapon until a more capable vehicle could be built. That vehicle would be the M10 gun motor carriage. Some even considered the M10 an expedient weapon. This image was part of the Camp Hood Story Series published by Barton Publishing.

In this rear view of the M3 gun motor carriage, the crew loads the breech of the 75-millimeter gun. The M3 was the first armored antitank weapon developed and used in combat in World War II. Its weaknesses were quickly realized, and it was replaced by the M10 gun motor carriage. This image was part of the Camp Hood Story Series.

An M10 gun motor carriage fires its main gun in action near St. Lo, France, in July 1944. The tank destroyers were quickly put to use after the invasion of Normandy. The one shown here is providing close support for the infantry. (Courtesy of the National Archives.)

This view of the live-fire section of the infiltration training course shows the machine gunner aiming over the heads of the soldiers. The soldier on the wooden platform is firing a .30-caliber machine gun approximately 24 inches above the heads of the soldiers crawling on the ground. Explosives and smoke were planted in the ground in fixed positions. This image was part of the story series published by Barton Publishing.

Soldiers from the Replacement Training Center in the 5th Regiment North Camp practice climbing up and down a cargo net. The net was created by post carpenters to train soldiers on how to disembark from ships into amphibious landing craft. This skill was needed for what was considered the most dangerous aspect of combat: the amphibious assault. The net would sway back and forth by the soldiers' movements, simulating open-water conditions and moderate seas. The net hangs from a 30-foot-high tower constructed in November 1943 as part of the 5th Regiment obstacle course.

These three M3 gun motor carriages were destroyed in the battle of Kasserine Pass in North Africa during the Tunisia campaign. This battle was a harsh lesson for the inexperienced US Army troops entering World War II. It was quickly evident that a better vehicle and better tactics were needed to face the German armor. It should also be noted that the tank destroyers were not utilized in the way they had been designed to be used. (Courtesy of the National Archives.)

An M10 tank destroyer of the 774th Battalion attached to the 94th Infantry Division on the west bank of the Rhine River carefully navigates the narrow streets of Petersen, Germany. The US Army had achieved its goal of a greatly expanded, well-trained, and superbly equipped force in a very short time. The villagers are waving white flags to show they are no threat.

# *Three*

# SPECIAL VISITORS AND EVENTS

Special events and special people were a common occurrence at Camp Hood, as tens of thousands of people created a continuous flow through the gates. Civilians and soldiers alike formed the personality of the early camp. Within 18 months of the start of post construction, housing for 80,000 soldiers had been completed. Some soldiers were there to train for combat, and some to sort mail or bake bread. All of the soldiers' and workers' roles were critical, and all personnel relied on each other to create an efficient camp that was meaningful and successful in its mission to help bring the war to a victorious close as quickly as possible. Some of the people looked at the camp as a temporary stopover for training. To these folks, Camp Hood was merely a place to endure and then move on, with the war waiting for them. Others saw the camp as a home and job and wanted to stay in the area and settle down. This mix of viewpoints was also sprinkled with welcome visitors, including the well-known and glamorous who came to entertain and show their patriotism. They brought special moments to those who were dedicated to the war effort and reminded them of the values they were fighting for.

The camp relied on the thousands of civilians who poured into the area to fill the needs of the camp's facilities. Advice was readily sought and used by the camp administration from the local populace. In appreciation for all the efforts of the civilians, Camp Hood hosted or sponsored recognition dances, threw parties, and handed out special awards for the civilian workers. There were USO camp shows, parades by soldiers in the towns, and even a special park donated to the soldiers by the town of Lampasas. The energy and cooperation aroused by the new camp and supported by the people around it created a thriving new community that would continue to endure over the years, to the present.

"This is Bob, Camp Hood, Hope" was broadcast on the airwaves all across America as Bob Hope hosted his popular radio variety show at Camp Hood on April 20, 1943. Hope brought his show to the camp during an incredible 12-month whirlwind tour that included visiting 42 military bases across the country. He started the tradition of camp shows on May 6, 1941, at March Field and never relented until December 1990. Shown here are, from left to right, Francis Langford, Bob

Hope, Barbara Jo Allen as Vera Vague, and Jerry Colonna, all regulars of *The Pepsodent Radio Show* on NBC. Also in the show that night were singer and bandleader Skinnay Ennis and the popular band Six Hits and a Miss. They played to a packed audience at the large field house in South Camp Hood.

Bob Hope brings a smile to the face of Camp Hood post commander Col. Charles Thirlkeld as he prepares to take the stage. Hope's success in relating to the troops was unparalleled. His tireless travels across the United States and in the different theaters of war created a USO tradition that still carries on today.

A young woman receives a civilian six-month award from Col. Charles M. Thirlkeld, Camp Hood's post commander. This type of award was intended to reward loyalty, add to morale, and boost productivity among the civilian workers on the post.

Right, Betty Smith speaks with post commander Charles M. Thirlkeld at the Christmas dance on December 18, 1943. She is receiving her prize as a winner of the Victory Suggestion Contest. The dance was held in the camp field house. All attempts were made to create a "civilian night club atmosphere with decorations and live music." Shown below is the Christmas sign painted by Pvt. Bob Cole of HQ Detachment DEML. The sign hung from one end of the building.

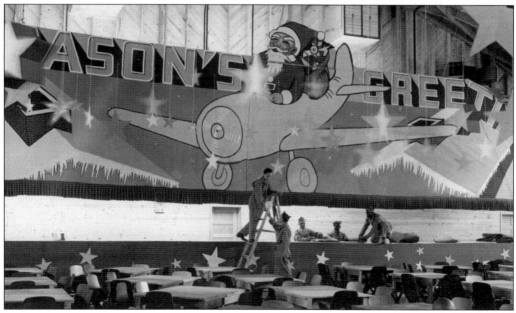

```
          MERRY CHRISTMAS TO THE CAMP CO

Breathes there a gal with soul so dead
Who never to herself hath said
I've worked so hard I'm nearly dead!

So, I'll just take off a moment or two
To discuss with my neighbor the contents of stew!
Lo and behold, no more than I do
But who's looking at Me but YOU.

You sort of glide in without a sound
And then my heart begins to pound,
I fumble for carbon, some paper or such,
But, darn it, I know you aren't missing much.

Its only a suggestion, but the way I feels
Is that you should tack these things on your heels
Then everytime you'd clomp in
Why I'd have work piled clear to my chin.

Seriously, though, you are kinda sweet,
Even if you are too light on your feet--
So, here's to a happy Christmas Day
And a New Year that's successful in every way.


                    Santa Claus
```

This is a light-hearted Christmas note to the camp commander from Santa Claus, or maybe the commander's staff. According to the note, it would appear that the commander was good at sneaking up on people when they least expected it. The letter was most likely given at a dinner or published in the *Hood Panther*.

Pictured here are, from left to right, Col. James A. Bethea, Texas governor Coke R. Stevenson, Gen. John H. Hester, and Col. C. M. Thirlkeld. In October 1943, Camp Hood soldiers attended a "meet the governor party" and a Friday-night dance with women at the Governor's Ball in Temple, held in the high school gymnasium. Civilian prizes were awarded, and music was provided by the First Tank Destroyer Band.

Comedian and musician Bob Burns broadcast his radio show, *The Bob Burns Show,* from the Camp Hood field house on June 10, 1943. Here, he shows off his invention and namesake instrument, the "Bazooka," at the camp. Burns built the instruments himself, usually making one for each show. The sound it emitted was compared to a wounded moose. By the end of each show, Burns would usually break the Bazooka into pieces. His homespun tales of fictional hillbilly relatives Uncle Fud and Aunt Doody kept audiences in stitches. Burns pointed out that his Bazooka discharged a racket, instead of a rocket. The Army's handheld rocket launcher was named after the famous instrument.

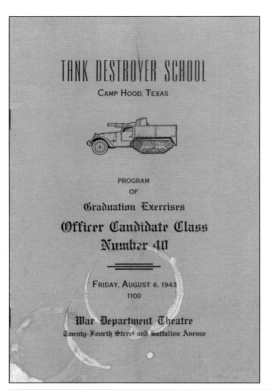

# TANK DESTROYER SCHOOL

CAMP HOOD, TEXAS

PROGRAM
OF

## Graduation Exercises

### Officer Candidate Class
### Number 40

FRIDAY, AUGUST 6, 1943
1100

**War Department Theatre**
Twenty-Fourth Street and Battalion Avenue

Shown at left is the cover of the program for the graduation of Officer Candidate Class No. 40 on August 6, 1943. Officer candidate classes were held at Camp Hood almost as soon as the camp opened and continued throughout the war. The classes, initially 13 weeks long, were later expanded to run 17 weeks. Lt. Col. E.J. Howell was the commanding officer of the Officer Candidate School regiment. There were approximately 85 candidates in each Officer Candidate School class. A new class was started every week. Shown below is the roster of the 40th Officer Candidate School class. One famous Camp Hood Officer Candidate School graduate was Louis L'Amour, the popular Western novelist.

**COMMANDING OFFICER, O. C. S. REGIMENT**

*E. J. Howell, Lt. Colonel, Infantry*

**COMPANY OFFICERS**

*Fourth Company, O. C. S. R.*

*Louis M. Jarosz, 1st Lt., AUS*
*Commanding Officer*

*Thomas F. Reed, 1st Lt., FA*          *Percy R. Peck, 2d Lt., FA*
*Herman J. Terbieten, 2d Lt., AUS*

**OFFICER CANDIDATE CLASS NO. 40**

| | | | |
|---|---|---|---|
| Allen, John M. | Hillman, James T. | Nitz, Ralph A. | Smith, James A., Jr. |
| Allison, Harold E. | Hintze, Walter C. | O'Hare, James P. | Spear, Lester K. |
| Alter, Edward | Hughes, Daniel A. | Olson, Charles A. | Spring, John J., Jr. |
| Apple, Charles F. | Hunter, Elmer C. | Paich, Joseph H. | Stagl, John M. |
| Bennett, Robert E. | Hutton, Asa J. | Park, William R. | Stevens, James W. |
| Brumagim, Duane T. | Jacobsen, Martin | Phillips, Dean K. | Stone, Calvin R. |
| Budd, John A. | Jacoby, Marshall L. | Roach, Ernest E. | Trelease, Robert H. |
| Chisholm, Roderick A. | Jordan, Jefferson L. | Rohrer, Melvin L. | Tuckerman, Chester W. |
| Cole, Byron M. | Joyce, Thomas, Jr. | Rosell, Alfred R. | Ward, Henry B., Jr. |
| Dahl, P. O., Jr. | Knight, Hale H. | Ryan, Mortimer S. | Wells, Frederick A. |
| De Pasquale, Charles A. | Kuhn, Clarence A. | Sekulich, John | Wienman, Alan M. |
| Fox, Carroll W. | Lawler, Robert W. | Shea, Ralph C. | Wiesbrock, Joseph W. |
| Francis, William B., Jr. | McKeown, Douglass O. | Smith, Frederick G. | Wishnick, Milton W. |
| Frey, Phalen S. | Meyer, Theodore O. | | |
| Hailey, Carl C. | Miller, Edward D. | Wolfe, Roger E. | |
| Hamann, Richard G. | Miller, Lem E. | | |
| Henry, Russell J. | Nickerson, Wendell R. | | |
| Hight, J. R., Jr. | Nielsen, Harry B. | | |

Red Skelton put on an intimate show for patients at the camp hospital. He was so impressed with a nurse, 1st Lt. Dorothea Engel, that he asked for her autograph. Engel, a Bataan heroine, was one of the last Army personnel evacuated from the island as the Japanese invaded. She said of her experience on Corregidor: "The morale of the nurses was wonderful. No one griped or complained. We were terribly frightened and we longed for peace and home, but none of us ever broke down and indulged in hysterics. It meant a great deal to the wounded and sick to have American women to give them the expert care their mothers and wives would have wanted for them." Arthur Miller wrote a play, *I Was Married on Bataan*, about her story and the tragic days of the fall of Manila.

Entertainer Red Skelton performs one of his crowd-pleasing bits in July 1943. He played to several sold-out audiences at the field house in South Camp and other locations around the camp. His show was fast-moving, and he recruited camp talent to help add local flavor to his skits.

Hedy Lamarr stands between Gen. John H. Hester, Tank Destroyer Center commanding general (center), and Col. Charles M. Thirlkeld, post commander (far right). Few people at the time knew that Lamar was an avid tinkerer and experienced inventor who held a highly technical patent involving spread spectrum radio technology. This technology is the basis for cellular phone communication used today. She tried to push this technology as a means of guiding torpedoes, but was rebuffed by the military brass in the War Department.

Hedy Lamarr arrives at the North Camp airstrip in January 1944 as part of the 8th Service Command theatrical conference, held at the camp.

*Hellzapoppin'*, with Joan Blondell, was performed at the Camp Hood field house on March 6, 1943. Blondell performed two shows that Saturday. She brought the Broadway musical comedy, created by Ole Oleson and Chic Jonson, to the camp, courtesy of the USO camp show system.

Above, Camp Hood officers attend a dinner in September 1942 at the Kyle Hotel in Temple, Texas. Seated at center is Gen. A.D. Bruce, commanding general of Camp Hood. His wife, Roberta, is on the left. Bruce was one of the founders of the tank destroyer doctrine. At right is Mrs. Thompson and Col. Harry F. Thompson. Shown below, also attending the dinner at the Kyle Hotel, is British army brigadier Piers Duncan Williams Dunn (center). On the right are Mrs. Ernest and Col. Herbert L. Earnest. Most likely, all are enjoying the view from the rooftop dining room of the hotel.

Others attending the dinner at the Kyle Hotel include, from left to right, Lt. Col. Wheaton (director of the automotive department), Mrs. Thirlkeld, Col. Charles M. Thirlkeld, unidentified, Maj. Kenneth McGregor, and Col. George Beatty (commanding officer of the Student Regiment).

Women's Army Corps (WACS) officer Lt. Col. Zita Callaghan, chief nurse of McCloskey General Hospital, and Colonel Bethea, commanding officer of the hospital, speak to a wounded soldier lying on a cot. McCloskey General Hospital became one of the largest Army general hospitals in the country. It is currently the site of a Veterans Administration hospital in the Temple area.

In December 1943, a farewell dinner was held for Col. James A. Murphy, the camp supply and service officer. He was leaving for Camp Barkeley, Texas. Murphy had served during the crucial and trying months of the camp's beginning, from March 1942 until December 1943. He was succeeded by Lt. Col. Abraham Tabachnik, former camp personnel officer. From left to right are Col. C.M. Thirlkeld, Colonel Murphy, Col. Donald R. Dunkle (executive officer of North Camp Hood), and Lt. Col. Tabachnik.

On September 2, 1943, the Brazilian minister of war, Gen. Eurico Gasper Dutra, visited Camp Hood. He was accompanied by eight of his staff. Shown above are, from left to right, an unidentified Brazilian officer, Maj. Gen. Orlando Ward, Maj. General Dutra, an unidentified US officer, and an unidentified Brazilian officer. Dutra later became the 16th president of Brazil in 1946. Below, the Brazilian team inspects an M10 tank destroyer. Most of the Brazilian armor was manufactured in the United States and given to Brazil under the Lend-Lease program.

This is the schedule for members of the Oil Workers International Union who stayed overnight at Camp Hood. This was a very special opportunity for civilians to experience tank destroyer training firsthand. They were placed under the command of Col. Wint Smith for a day and experienced some of the special combat training at the camp. They were even allowed to fire large-caliber weapons and run through the village course.

At times, church services were held in the field. Shown here is a well-attended Easter service under pleasant skies at Camp Hood around 1944. Many services were held under similar conditions in the theater of war in Europe and the Pacific.

OIL WORKERS INTERNATIONAL UNION OF C.I.O.
VISIT TO CAMP HOOD, TEXAS
(Home of the Tank Destroyers)
Amended Schedule

I.  Schedule of Activities - August 5, 1943.

    1700 - Arrive Camp Hood. Address of Welcome by Colonel Charles Thirlkeld, Commanding Officer, Camp Hood.
    1715 - Taken to Headquarters 635th TD Bn, Lt. Col. Wint Smith, Commanding. Issued coveralls, shoes, helmets. Messed and quartered.
    2015 - Leave 635th TD Bn for Battle Conditioning Course #2.
    2030 - Arrive Battle Conditioning Course #2. Major Sleator in charge. Actual participation in the conditioning of soldiers for night fighting.
    2400 - Return to 635th TD Bn and quarters.

II.  Schedule of Activities - August 6, 1943.

    0555 - Reveille
    0630 - Breakfast, policing quarters and bunks.
    0720 - Police call.
    0745 - Leave for Battle Conditioning Course #3.
    0800 - 1000 Battle Conditioning Course #3. Major Sleator in charge. Close combat firing; Nazi Village fighting; H. E. firing -- 5 rounds at mock tank.
    1015 - Arrive Jack Mountain Gas Car Range.
    1015 - 1045 Six members are turned over to Colonel Buchwald, 605th TD Bn to fire M-10.
    1045 - 1130 Gun maintenance.
    1015 - 1045 Other members under Colonel Smith, 635th TD Bn to fire 3" towed guns.
    1045 - 1130 Gun maintenance.
    1200 - Arrive at 635th Bn mess.
    1245 - Leave for School area.
    1300 - Address by General Mayberry, Commandant TDS, at Classroom #21.
    1315 - 1430 Inspection of automotive, weapons and other installations of School.
    1430 - Leave in trucks for Service of Supply.
    1445 - Ordnance Branch.
    1530 - Quartermaster Branch.
    1700 - Return to 635th Hqs to turn in equipment and clean up.
    1800 - Load baggage in bus, 635th Bn Hqs at 50th Street and Battalion Avenue.
    1815 - Supper at Service Clubs.
    1930 - Leave Camp Hood for Fort Worth from 37th Street Service Club.

Colonel Wint Smith, Commanding Officer 635th TD Bn will be your Commanding Officer while here; Colonel Buchwald, Commanding Officer, 605th TD Bn will show you the M-10; Major Sleator, Director of Battle Conditioning Course, Captains F. D. King and G. H. Meyers, Assistants; Lieutenant Mayborn, Post PRO.

WACS members from the 1848th Unit, 8th Service Command, are greeted by their commanding officer, Col. Charles Thirlkeld. WACS served in the branch of Army Service Forces. In this case, the WACS were assigned to the 8th Service area, which covered Texas. By 1944, the women of WACS were not needed to replace men who were going to be sent over, but were needed to replace men who were already gone. WACS started as WAACS, an auxiliary group, on May 15, 1942. The initial volunteers received less pay than the men and received no benefits.

WAACS members graduate to the WACS service as they take their oath at Camp Hood. The Army officially converts the Women's Army Auxiliary Corps to full status as the Women's Army Corps on July 1, 1943. Approximately 150,000 women served during World War II, releasing the equivalent of seven divisions of men for combat. The women who volunteered for service had to overcome hostility at the sight of women in uniform, both inside and outside the military. Yet, many generals in the high command stated that women were the best soldiers they had. Douglas MacArthur said, "they worked harder, complained less, and were better disciplined than men." WACS was disbanded in 1978, as women were fully integrated into the Army.

Officer Candidate School graduate Charles "Chuck" M. Thirlkeld Jr. receives his second lieutenant bars. He is flanked by Col. Charles M. Thirlkeld, post commander, and Mary Thirlkeld. Chuck Thirlkeld, who graduated in the 32nd OCS class at Camp Hood, went on to the 101st Airborne Division, 506th Parachute Infantry Regiment, 2nd Battalion, HQ Company, attached to an antitank platoon with Easy Company. During the Ardennes offensive, also known as the Battle of the Bulge, Thirlkeld was struck and killed during a German artillery and rocket barrage around 4:00 p.m. on January 3, 1945. The location of the incident is memorialized in the book *Band of Brothers* as the Bois Jacques, south of the Foy area. Thirlkeld was working with a bazooka squad and was standing next to Lt. "Buck" Lynn D. Compton when he was struck.

# *Four*

# CAMP EXPANSION

Camp Hood grew at a tremendous pace in its first year. The pressures on Camp Hood and its surrounding environs to add more training facilities were immediately felt as the war effort expanded and the number of soldiers in the US Army grew fortyfold from prewar levels. An additional 34,943 acres were purchased in Coryell County, between the existing camp and what was then called the subcamp about six miles from Gatesville. In addition, 16,000 acres were purchased in Bell County for tank destroyer use. After the new acreage was added, the entire camp encompassed approximately 160,000 acres, making Camp Hood one of the largest bases in the United States. Some of the most pressing needs included a Tank Destroyer Basic Unit Training Center, Infantry Replacement Training Center, Tank Destroyer Replacement Training Center, the Southern Branch of the United States Disciplinary Barracks, and a prisoner-of-war facility. There was always a demand for qualified instructors and officers. This need was hard to fill at times. The Infantry Replacement Center was activated on March 10, 1944. The prisoner-of-war camps for Germans were built in May 1943. They were designed to hold 3,000 prisoners at the North Camp and 1,000 at the South Camp. The camp population increased to 90,000 troops in 1943. The National Housing Authority built two towns to house the civilians needed to work at the camp.

The mission of the camp changed by early 1944 as the need for infantrymen outstripped the need for tank destroyer men. As German tank forces dwindled, it became apparent that the anticipated number of antitank battalions would not be needed. The US Army ended up never facing the large Panzer formations used by Germany at the beginning of the war. The Army always needed infantrymen, and the Infantry Replacement Training Center took precedence over the Tank Destroyer Training Center. By September 1944, the Infantry Replacement Center was the largest activity on the post, with a population of over 31,000 troops.

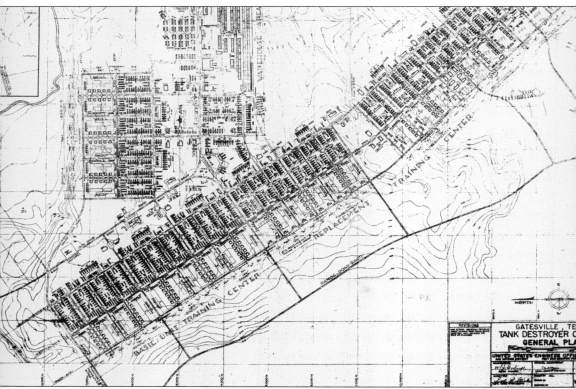

This is an original diagram of the general plan of the North Camp Hood expansion, as drawn on February 8, 1943. This cantonment was only a few miles from Gatesville and approximately 18 miles from South Camp Hood. The north cantonment was divided into two sections, a Replacement Training Center side and the Basic Unit Training Center side. Approximately 60,000 acres were purchased to facilitate this expansion. Augmenting these sections were a post hospital, a prisoner-of-war camp, and additional training grounds and firing ranges. A railhead area and warehouse area were also included in the cantonment to facilitate logistical supply.

The second formal flag-raising ceremony at Camp Hood was held on May 29, 1943, as the North Camp Hood Cantonment officially opened. Gen. Leslie McNair said at the opening of the North Camp, "I know of no war training agency which was conceived, planned, built and put into full operation with greater speed, skill and soundness than Camp Hood."

As Camp Hood grew, so did its leadership. Shown here are some of the generals and colonels in charge at the Tank Destroyer Center. They are, from left to right, Gen. Orlando C. Ward, Gen. Hugh Mayberry, Gen. Richard Tindall, Gen. Walter Dumas, an unidentified colonel, Col. Donald Dunkle, Col. Charles Thirlkeld, and Col. George Beatty.

The opening of the North Camp coincided with Gen. Orlando C. Ward assuming command of the Tank Destroyer Center. Lt. Gen. Leslie McNair, commanding general of all Army ground forces, attended the opening ceremonies. Here, Ward (right) and McNair pose after watching the review parade. Ward brought battlefield experience from the first US combat operations in North Africa.

Gen. McNair (right) and Gen. Ward use an M3 gun motor carriage as a reviewing stand as the troops of Camp Hood pass in review. Using gun motor carriages in this manner was standard practice at Camp Hood for parades. Several review parades a week were held at the camp.

Gen. Leslie McNair (center) is flanked on the left by General Mayberry and on the right by General Ward. They are enjoying their simple breakfast in the officer's mess as McNair visits for the opening of the North Camp in May 1943.

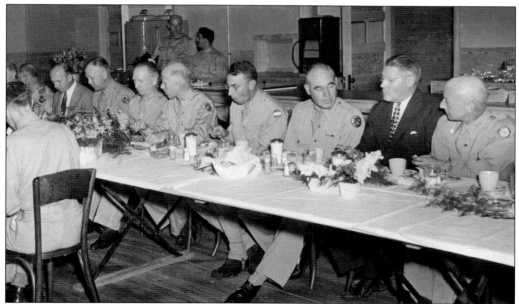

This is another view of the celebratory breakfast for the opening of the North Camp. At far right, Colonel Thirlkeld exhibits the white-on-blue shoulder patch of the Army Services Command. Third from right, General Thompson wears the tank destroyer shoulder patch, depicting a panther with a tank in its jaws. To Thompson's right is an unidentified colonel with the red, white, and blue horizontal striped Army Ground Forces patch.

Lt. Gen. Leslie McNair (left) awards the Army Distinguished Service Cross to camp commanding general Orlando Ward. Ward commanded the 1st Armored Division during Operation Torch in North Africa. Ward assisted Chief of Staff George Marshall in the difficult buildup and preparation of the Army before the war. Ward earned a Purple Heart when he was wounded in the eye in Tunisia in a night assault on the Meknessy Heights. Other awards included the Silver Star with oak leaf cluster, the Army Distinguished Service Medal, and the Legion of Merit with oak leaf cluster.

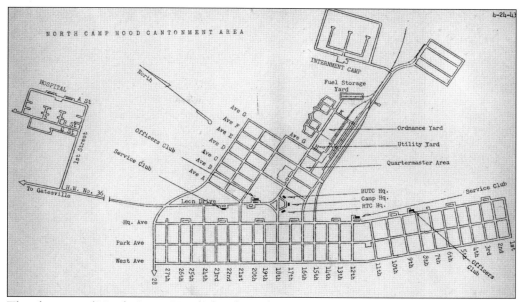

This diagram of North Camp Hood, dated April 4, 1943, shows the officers clubs and enlisted service clubs. The diagram also shows the location of the headquarters campus for the three major training components of the North Camp. The prisoner-of-war internment camp can be seen at the top. The internment camp held 3,000 prisoners. Another internment camp at South Camp held another 1,000 prisoners.

The headquarters for the Tank Destroyer Replacement Training Center was located at North Camp Hood, on the same campus as the Basic Unit Training Center and the Advanced Unit Training Center. This unit was responsible for training soldiers to fill empty spots in existing tank destroyer battalions. These empty spots resulted from soldiers who fell out of the battalion due to illness, accident, or death in combat.

The headquarters for the Tank Destroyer Basic Training Unit (BTU) opened at the camp on May 1, 1943. Conducting basic training at Camp Hood was viewed as a necessity, due to the lack of abilities of the soldiers in the new units arriving at Camp Hood for advanced training. Many of the members of the new units had a lack of small-weapons experience, and there was a shortage of personnel and experienced officers. The BTU was able to bring all new groups coming in up to an acceptable level of ability to start their advanced training. The BTU would also fill out training units and make sure they were at full strength. It also allowed officers in the newly arriving units time to understand the tank destroyer doctrine. The Basic Unit Training Center would be renamed the Individual Unit Training Center.

The headquarters building for the North Camp is shown here. When Maj. Gen. Orlando Ward assumed command of the Tank Destroyer Center, organizations and expansion had been achieved. The center thereafter focused on its training and development mission.

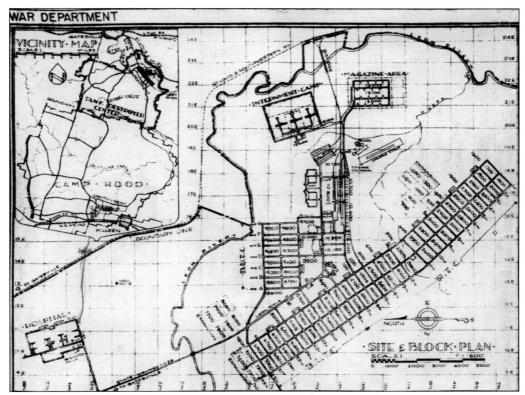

This site block plan was drawn in February 1943. It shows the relation of north and south cantonments in the upper left. The camps were just far enough apart to warrant replicating many of the post facilities. Each camp had a post exchange or store and its own officer clubs and enlisted service clubs. South Camp had the only large field house for entertainment.

This early aerial photograph of North Camp Hood, taken around 1943, shows the Replacement Training Center section in the foreground. The basic road structure has been laid out. A lot of the buildings are still absent in this view. The railroad yard is just getting under way on the right. The street grid for the new hospital complex can be seen at upper right. With the completion of North Camp Hood, the organization and expansion of the Tank Destroyer Center was accomplished. The headquarters of the Replacement Training Center, the Basic Unit Training Center, and Advanced Unit Training Center were all on one campus. There was now room to house 80,000 troops.

This village was constructed in 1943 to house civilian workers and their families at Camp Hood. The plan included 1,091 units with 2,367 bedrooms. In the center of the complex were a school, a three-acre park, and a community building. The community was built by the National Housing Agency. All the units came furnished, with utilities provided. The trailer park, with a capacity for 385 units, was adjacent to the civilian village.

The Camp Hood trailer camp (pictured) was next to the civilian village. As civilians continued to pour into the area, more housing was needed. Lampasas Road separated the trailer camp from Camp Hood. There were 385 trailers in the camp. All utilities were provided by the Camp Hood internal utility service.

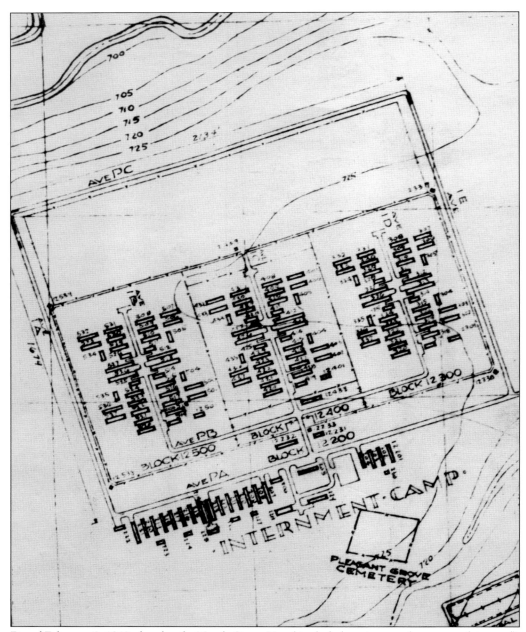

Dated February 8, 1943, the plan for North Camp Hood included a prisoner-of-war camp (pictured). This camp was designed to hold 3,000 prisoners. According to the Geneva Convention, prisoners were to be held in camps with similar climate to where they were captured. However uncomfortable, the POW camps were sometimes considered too comfortable for the captive Germans, and many a Texas community called its local camp the "Fritz Ritz." It was deemed that Texas had a climate similar to North Africa, so many members of Germany's Africa Korps were placed there. Discipline among the prisoners was rigidly enforced by the German officers and sergeants. The prisoners were amazed at the food available to them. Items such as meat, real coffee, and milk were extremely scarce and, in some cases, had not been tasted in years.

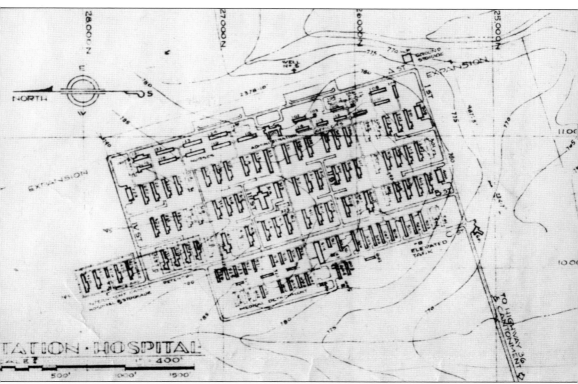

The general plan for the station hospital, located in the North Camp, is shown here. The name "station hospital" was common at most Army bases in the 1940s. The hospital was part of the overall Camp Hood expansion. The station hospital comprised 1,139 beds. It provided immediate aid to those training near Gatesville, eliminating the need to transport the injured all the way to McClosky Army General Hospital in Temple. The Red Cross assisted relatives of the wounded while visiting at the hospital and helped with transportation and housing of relatives during their stay.

Shown here are Lt. Gen. Leslie McNair (left), commanding general of Army Ground Forces, and Maj. Gen. Orlando Ward. McNair was responsible for the training of Army ground forces and all support services. He managed the incredible fortyfold increase in the size of the Army and of the training and support facilities. His staff also determined the numbers of men and equipment in both the armor and infantry divisions that were sent overseas. McNair pushed the concepts of a mobile army with the best equipment available. On July 25, 1944, while crouching in a foxhole anticipating a massive air bombardment near St. Lo, France, McNair was struck and killed by a bomb dropped by friendly forces.

*Five*

# THE WAR'S END

The primary mission of Camp Hood changed dramatically toward the end of World War II. Antitank warfare doctrine had run its course, as the German Panzer divisions fell apart and concentrated tank warfare was no longer occurring. No new Tank Destroyer Battalions were to be started. Camp Hood ended up sending 100 battalions into combat. The camp trained more than 300,000 troops in three years.

Camp Hood changed its primary training mission by focusing resources on enlarging the Infantry Replacement Training Center and shrinking the Tank Destroyer School footprint. The replacement center trained 56,313 troops from 1944 until the end of the war. After Germany capitulated on May 8, 1945, the offensive focus of the War Department turned solely on the conflict in the Pacific. The Japanese military was reeling from repeated losses, as island after island fell to the United States. The War Department was concerned about high troop losses, knowing the Japanese were going to defend the home islands vigorously and would most likely be using the method of defense exhibited on the various islands in the Pacific. It was determined that new offensive methods were needed to cope with the underground bunkers and tunnels used by Japanese defenders. Project Sphinx was approved by the War Department to develop offensive combat methods to thwart the Japanese. Because its terrain resembled that of Okinawa, Camp Hood was chosen as the location for Project Sphinx. More than 3,000 caves, spider holes, tunnels, and pillboxes were constructed in and around Manning Mountain and Clabber Point by civilians and German POWs. On August 5, 1945, a full report was delivered to the War Department summarizing the Scorpion outcomes. Japan capitulated on August 14, 1945, thus ending the war.

Camp Hood's future was in doubt as a permanent base. The cost of upgrading North Camp Hood ($32 million) was deemed too expensive, and the facility was shut down. South Camp was retained, and Camp Hood entered a new chapter in its history. From 1946 to 1950, the camp changed very little. Effective April 15, 1950, Camp Hood became Fort Hood and thus permanent in purpose and name.

Tank destroyer soldiers and infantrymen ride an M10 gun motor carriage through the German countryside as the end of the war in Europe neared. The men operating this M10 trained at Camp Hood, part of the 100 tank destroyer battalions sent into combat from the training grounds in Texas. With the tank threat almost eliminated, no new tank destroyer battalions were being trained. (Courtesy of the National Archives.)

Camp Hood soldiers admire the latest clothes and shoe fashions in town on June 7, 1945. The soldiers, having worn uniforms for the last few years, are ready to try their hands at civilian clothes again. Discussions were under way at this time on the future of tank destroyer operations in a peacetime environment.

The three tank destroyer gun motor carriages most commonly associated with Camp Hood are on display in a field at the camp about late 1943. The evolution of the weapons can be clearly seen when they are positioned side by side. They are, from left to right, the M18 Hellcat, the M10, and the M3 gun motor carriage. All three vehicle types were field-tested, used for training, and deployed from Camp Hood.

VOL. III        CAMP HOOD, TEX., JUNE 7, 1945.        NO. 25

Shown here is the new masthead of the camp newspaper. The publication evolved with the post. As the role of the tank destroyers lessened, and the Infantry Training Center gained in prominence, the name of the newspaper was changed. The tank destroyer panther symbol was removed, along with the name *Hood Panther*. The paper's name was changed to the *Camp Hood News*, reflecting the broader diversity of missions the camp had taken on. The many articles about tank destroyers and their exploits overseas in the paper were greatly watered down, in favor of more general articles about the infantry.

Lt. Gen. Ernest J. Dawley replaced General Hester as commander of the Tank Destroyer Center on June 26, 1944. Dawley saw combat in Operation Avalanche in Sicily with the Fifth Army prior to taking command at Camp Hood. He continued the training concepts of Hester, but with more focus on speed in gunnery and hitting power. General Dawley strongly recommended making the tank destroyer battalions organic to infantry components. He felt this would allow better inherent coordination of all resources. (Courtesy of the National Archives.)

Brig. Gen. Alexander O. Gorder replaced General Dawley on March 18, 1945, as the Tank Destroyer Training Center commander. Gorder's prior role at the camp was as the commanding general of the Tank Destroyer Replacement Training Center. General Gorder made a recommendation to the Army Ground Forces staff on June 15, 1945, to conduct tactical testing at North Camp Hood to develop means and materiel to use against Japanese defensive fortifications and underground tunnels. The War Department issued a directive on June 26, 1945, to create a secret "Sphinx" detachment, made up of 3,500 troops at Camp Hood, to conduct the testing. By August 5, 1945, a full report was delivered to Army Ground Forces leadership. Gorder would be the last Tank Destroyer Center commander, as the tank destroyer organization would cease to exist at the war's end. (Courtesy of Gorder.com.)

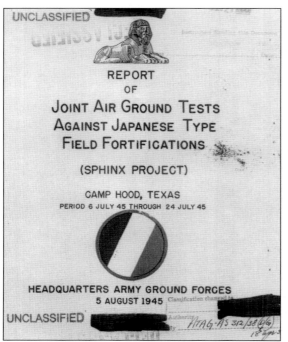

REPORT
OF
JOINT AIR GROUND TESTS
AGAINST JAPANESE TYPE
FIELD FORTIFICATIONS

(SPHINX PROJECT)

CAMP HOOD, TEXAS
PERIOD 6 JULY 45 THROUGH 24 JULY 45

HEADQUARTERS ARMY GROUND FORCES
5 AUGUST 1945 Classification changed to

Authority
MAG-AS 312/38 (6G)

Shown here is the Sphinx Project report cover page, dated August 5, 1945. The secret project was the last important contribution provided by the Tank Destroyer Center at Camp Hood. The project ran from July 6 to July 24, 1945. The Sphinx Project was devised to create effective ground and air support in attacking fortified Japanese positions. The War Department was concerned about the high casualty rate experienced at Iwo Jima and Leyte. A total of 3,500 troops participated at North Camp Hood in the project. German prisoners were used to dig caves, construct pill boxes, and create spider holes. The project was considered a success, as many new offensive techniques were developed. The war with Japan ended 10 days after the final Sphinx report was submitted on August 5, 1945. (Courtesy of the National Archives.)

A parade moves through the original Camp Hood. The streets are lined with barracks built to last just as long as the war. The old Camp Hood, with its whitewashed barracks and hard-packed roads, was soon to be no more. The temporary buildings would be torn down as they wore down, and improvements meant to make the post a permanent place would spring up to create what is now Fort Hood.

Around 1950, workers take down the word "Camp" as Camp Hood becomes Fort Hood. The tank destroyer panther emblem, now long gone, was replaced by the triangle of the 2nd Armored Division. The experiment of tank destroyer doctrine had run its course. Camp Hood became the permanent home to the 2nd Armored Division after the war. With North Camp gone, South Camp stayed relatively unchanged until the base was made permanent in 1950. (Courtesy of the National Archives.)

This is a newly built, open, light-filled barracks at Fort Hood around early 1950. The spacious windows give the barracks a "glassed-in" appearance to passing observers. After the war, due to a scarcity of funds, building improvements were sparse on the post. When the post became permanent, the World War II–era buildings were slowly torn down. Many new buildings, such as the barracks pictured here, were constructed in the 1950s. Many of the structures built during the war were constructed to last only about five years. (Courtesy of the National Archives.)

# DISCOVER THOUSANDS OF LOCAL HISTORY BOOKS FEATURING MILLIONS OF VINTAGE IMAGES

Arcadia Publishing, the leading local history publisher in the United States, is committed to making history accessible and meaningful through publishing books that celebrate and preserve the heritage of America's people and places.

Find more books like this at
## www.arcadiapublishing.com

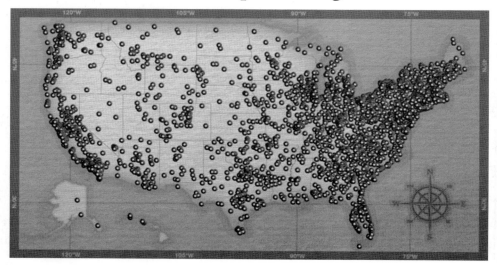

Search for your hometown history, your old stomping grounds, and even your favorite sports team.

Consistent with our mission to preserve history on a local level, this book was printed in South Carolina on American-made paper and manufactured entirely in the United States. Products carrying the accredited Forest Stewardship Council (FSC) label are printed on 100 percent FSC-certified paper.

MADE IN THE USA